BILLIE EILISH
GUITAR
29 POPULAR SONGS
FOR BEGINNERS & INTERMEDIATE

Billie Eilish Guitar Songbook: 29 Popular Songs for Beginners & Intermediate Players (Chords, Lyrics & Easy Arrangements)

This book contains simplified, educational arrangements of copyrighted songs for guitar, including chords, and lyrics.

Each piece has been carefully arranged to help beginner and intermediate guitarists learn, practice, and perform Billie Eilish's music in a clear, accessible, and inspiring way.

Cassiel Dass

THANK YOU!

This book came from a simple love for music. We put a lot of effort and heart into it, hoping to make something that can truly help you grow your skills while enjoying every song you play. I really hope this book feels worth it for you, and that it brings you the same joy we felt while making it.

Cassiel Dass

MORE TO KNOW ABOUT THIS BOOK

This book includes 29 Billie Eilish songs arranged with easy and intermediate chords, clear lyrics, and simple strumming patterns. Each page shows the chord diagrams you need, making it easy to follow and play.

You might find a very slight difference in some lyrics, only to make the rhythm flow better with guitar sound. Everything was made to help you learn fast, sound good, and enjoy every song from start to finish.

Table of contents 🎼

Birds of a Feather

Music by Billie Eilish

CHORDS

D   Bm7   Em7   A7sus4

STRUMMING PATTERN

WHOLE SONG 105 bpm

1 & 2 & 3 & 4 &

[Verse 1]
D
 I want you to stay
            Bm7
'Til I'm in the grave
            Em7
'Til I rot away, dead and buried
            A7sus4
'Til I'm in the casket you carry
                    D
If you go, I'm goin' too, uh

[Verse 2]
                Bm7
'Cause it was always you, uh
                Em7
And if I'm turnin' blue, please
don't save me
            A7sus4
Nothin' left to lose without my
baby

[Refrain]
D
 Birds of a feather, we should
stick together, I know
Bm7
   I said I'd never think I
wasn't better alone

Em7
   Can't change the weather, might
not be forever
        A7sus4
But if   it's forever, it's even
 better

[Pre-Chorus]
D
 And I don't know what I'm cryin'
 Bm7
 for

I don't think I could love you more
Em7

It might not be long, but baby, I
A7sus4

I'll love you 'til the day that I
    D
die

[Chorus]
                        Bm7
'Til the day that I die
                        Em7
'Til the light leaves my eyes
                A7sus4
'Til the day that I die

1

```
                 D
I want you to see, hmm                    I love you, don't act so surprised
                                          A7sus4

[Verse 3]
              Bm7                         [Outro]
How you look to me, hmm                   D Bm7 Em7 A7sus4
                 Em7
You wouldn't believe if I told ya
                    A7sus4
You would keep the compliments I
throw ya
                         D
But you're so full of shit, uh


[Verse 4]
              Bm7
Tell me it's a bit, oh
                      Em7
Say you don't see it, your mind's
polluted
                 A7sus4
Say you wanna quit, don't be stupid


[Pre-Chorus]
D
 And I don't know what I'm cryin'
 Bm7
 for

I don't think I could love you more
Em7

Might not be long, but baby, I
A7sus4
Don't wanna say goodbye


[Chorus]
D
                           Bm7
'Til the day that I die
                             Em7
'Til the light leaves my eyes
                   A7sus4 D
'Til the day that I die


[Post-Chorus]
                    Bm7
I knew you in another life

You had that same look in your eyes
Em7


                   2
```

Wildflower

Music by Billie Eilish

CHORDS

Dmaj7	C#m7	F#m	E	C#7	A

(chord diagrams)

STRUMMING PATTERN

WHOLE SONG 74 bpm

↓   ↓   ↑   ↑ ↓   ↓   ↓ ↑
1   &   2   &   3   &   4   &

[Intro]
Dmaj7 C#m7 F#m

[Verse 1]
Dmaj7   **C#m7**
     Things fall apart
                   F#m
And time breaks your heart
I wasn't there but I know
Dmaj7   **C#m7**
     She was your girl
                 F#m
You showed her the world

You fell out of love And you both
   E
let
   Dmaj7
go

[Pre-Chorus]
                  C#m7
She was cryin' in my shoulder
                F#m
All I could do was hold her
Only made us closer
   E
Until July
Dmaj7
     And I know that you love me
C#m7

                 F#m
You don't need to remind me
I should put it all behind me
Shouldn't I?

[Chorus]
   Dmaj7   **E**
But I   see her in the back of my
 mind
    C#7   **F#m E**   **Dmaj7**
All the time   like a fever
       E   **C#7**
Like I'm burnin' alive like a sign
F#m
       E   **Dmaj7**   **C#m7**
Did I cross the line? Mm
   F#m A
Mm

[Verse 2]
Dmaj7
     Well, good things don't last
C#m7
                F#m
And life moves so fast
                   E
I'd never ask who was better
Dmaj7   **C#m7**
     'Cause she couldn't be
               F#m
More different from me

```
                              E Dmaj7
Happy and free in leather


[Pre-Chorus]
                                      C#m7
And I know that you love me
                                      F#m
You don't need to remind me
Put it all behind me
      E
But, baby


[Chorus]
  Dmaj7                     E
I      see her in the back of my
mind
      C#7      F#m E              Dmaj7
All the time     feels like a fever
          E                    C#7
Like I'm burnin' alive like a  sign
F#m
      E              Dmaj7
Did I cross the line?


[Post-Chorus]
                  E
You say no one knows you so well
    C#7
But every time you touch me,
      F#m               E
I just wonder how she felt
Dmaj7                     E
Valentines Day cryin' in the hotel
            C#7
I know you didn't mean to hurt me,
     F#m
So I kept it to myself
                  E
And I wonder


[Outro 1]
        Dmaj7
Do you see  her in
     E
The back of your mind?
    C#7      F#m
In my eyes


[Outro 2 (Fade In)]
Dmaj7 E C#7 F#m E
```

```
Dmaj7                         E
You  say no one knows you so well
      C#7
But every time you touch me,
        F#m           E
I just wonder how she felt
Dmaj7                     E
Valentines Day cryin' in the hotel
            C#7
I know you didn't mean to hurt me,
      F#m
So I kept it to myself
```

4

Chihiro

Music by Billie Eilish

CHORDS

Cmaj7   Am7   Em7   Gmaj7

STRUMMING PATTERN

WHOLE SONG 110 bpm

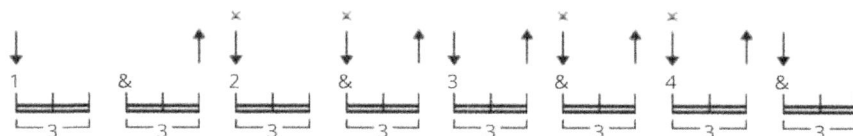

[Verse 1]
Cmaj7
    To take my love away
Am7
   When I come back around
Will I know what to say?
Em7
    Said you won't forget my name
      Gmaj7
Not today, not tomorrow
       Cmaj7
Kind of   strange
Feeling sorrow
      Am7
I got   change
You could borrow
Em7
   When I come back around
Will I know what to say?
      Gmaj7
Not today, maybe tomorrow

[Pre-Chorus]
Cmaj7
Open up the door, can you open up
the door?
  Am7
I know you said before you can't
cope with any more
    Em7
You told me it was war, said you'd
show me what's in store

Gmaj7
I hope it's not for sure, can you
open up the door?

[Chorus]
   Cmaj7 Am7
Did you   take
    Em7   Gmaj7
My love away
      Cmaj7 Am7
From me?   Me
Em7   Gmaj7
   Me

[Verse 2]
Cmaj7
    Saw your seat at the counter
when I looked away
Am7
   Saw you turned around, but
it wasn't your face
      Em7
Said I   need to be alone now, I'm
taking a break
       Gmaj7
How comÐµ when I   returned, you
wÐµre gone away?

[Bridge]

5

```
Cmaj7
I don't, I don't know
      Am7
Why I called
                      Em7
I don't know you at all
            Gmaj7
I don't know you, no, I don't
   Cmaj7
I don't, I don't know
        Am7
What I thought
                      Em7
I don't know you at all
            Gmaj7
I don't know you


[Chorus]
        Cmaj7  Am7
Did you    take
   Em7     Gmaj7
My love away
        Cmaj7  Am7
From me?    Me
Em7 Gmaj7
        And that's when you found
me


[Verse 3]
Cmaj7                          Am7
      I was waiting in the garden
                          Em7
Contemplating, beg your pardon

But there's a part of me that
              Gmaj7
recognizes you
Do you feel that too?
            Cmaj7
When you told me it was serious
            Am7
Were you serious? Mm
              Em7
They told me they were only curious
            Gmaj7
Now it's serious? Mm


[Pre-Chorus]
Cmaj7
Open up the door, can you open up
the door?
```

```
Am7
I know you said before you can't
cope with any more
        Em7
You told me it was war, said you'd
show me what's in store
   Gmaj7
I hope it's not for sure, can you
open up the door?


[Chorus]
Cmaj7 Am7 Em7 Gmaj7 Cmaj7
                      Running my
hands up my lap
            Am7
And you tell me it's all been a
trap
              Em7
And you don't know if you'll make
it back
              Gmaj7
I said, "No, don't say that"


[Outro]
Cmaj7
Running my hands up my lap
            Am7
And you tell me it's all been a
trap
              Em7
And you don't know if you'll make
it back
              Gmaj7
I said, "No, don't say that"
Cmaj7
Running my hands up my lap
            Am7
And you tell me it's all been a
trap
              Em7
And you don't know if you'll make
it back
              Gmaj7
I said, "No, don't say that"
Cmaj7
      Mhm
```

The Greatest

Music by Billie Eilish

CHORDS

STRUMMING PATTERN

WHOLE SONG 66 bpm

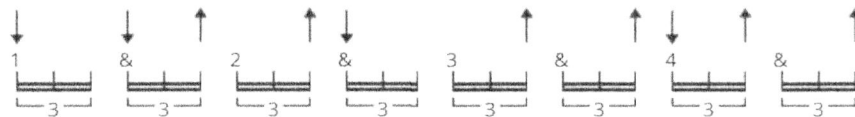

[Verse 1]

        Am7
I'm trying my best

          Gmaj7
To keep you satisfied

        Am7
Let you get your   rest

         Gmaj7
While I stayed up all   night

        Am7
And you don't wanna know

[Pre-Chorus]

        Emadd9
How alone I've   been

Gmaj7   Am7
   Let you come and   go

        Emadd9   D
Whatever I state I'm   in, ah

[Chorus]

Cadd9
Man, am I the greatest?

Em7
My congratulations

D
All my love and patience

Cadd9   Em
All my admiration

Am7
All the times I waited

    Em7
For you to want me naked

D
Made it all look painless

C
Man, am I the greatest?

[Bridge]

Am7
  Ohoh

  Gmaj7
Ohoh

Mm

        Am7
Doing what's right

[Verse 2]

        Gmaj7
Without a reward

```
                      Am7
And we don't have to    fight
                            Gmaj7
When it's not worth fighting  for
Mm
                      Am7
And you don't wanna know


[Pre-Chorus]
                    Emadd9 Gmaj7
What I would've done        mm
            Am7
Anything at   all
                Emadd9
Worse than anyone
D
Mm, ooh


[Chorus]
Cadd9
Man, am I the greatest?
Em7
My congratulations
D
All my love and patience
Cadd9              Em
All  my admiration
Am7
All the times I waited
      Em7
For you to want me naked
   D
I made it all look painless
C                       F
Man, am I the greatest?


[Interlude]
C           G
 The greatest
      F
Hey, hey
          C       G
The greatest, ahoh
Ahahah, ahah
    F
I, I
          C
I loved you and I still do
G
 Just wanted passion from you
                        F
Just wanted what I gave you
```

```
              C          Em A
I've waited and waited    Oh


[Outro]
C
Man, am I the greatest?
Em
   God, I hate it
D
All my love and patience
C            Em
Unappreciated
     Am7
You said your heart was jaded
       Em
You could'nt even break it
    D
I should'nt have to say it
      C
You could have been the greatest
```

8

Lunch

Music by Billie Eilish

CHORDS

```
  Bm          Em          A           G           F#m
 x      2fr                x                              2fr
 ┌┬┬┬┐       ┌┬┬┬┐       ┌┬┬┬┐       ┌┬┬┬┐       ┌┬┬┬┐
 │││││       │●●││       │●●●│       │●│││       │●●││
 │●●●│       │││││       │││││       ││●●│       │││││
 │││││       │││││       │││││       │││││       │││││
  342         12          123        21  34       34
```

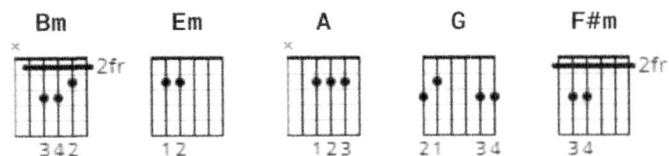

STRUMMING PATTERN

WHOLE SONG 125 bpm

```
↓    ↓    ↓  ↑      ↑
1  & 2  & 3  & 4  &
```

[Intro]
Bm
   Oh mmm

[Chorus]
Em   Bm
  I could eat that girl for lunch
          Em
Yeah, she dances on my tongue
          Bm
Tastes like she might be the one
Em   Bm
  And I could never get enough
       A
I could buy her so much stuff
     G   F#m   Em
It's a craving, not a crush, uh
Bm
Call me when you're there
      Em
Said, "I bought you something rare"
     Bm
And I left it under "Claire"
Em   Bm
  So now she's coming up the stairs
     A
So I'm pulling up a chair
     G   F#m
And I'm putting up my hair

[Verse 1]

Em   Bm
  Baby, I think you were made for
me
Em   Bm
  Somebody write down the recipe
Em   Bm
  Been trying hard not to overeat
A   G   F#m
 You're just so sweet
Em   Bm
  I'll run a shower for you like
      Em
you want
          Bm
Clothes on the counter for you, try
     Em
'em on
       Bm
If I'm allowed, I'll have you take
     A G F#m
'em off
Huh

[Chorus]
Em   Bm
  I could eat that girl for lunch
         Em
Yeah, she dances on my tongue
         Bm
Tastes like she might be the one
Em   Bm
  And I could never get enough

9

```
                A
I could buy her so much stuff
           G              F#m
It's a craving, not a crush, uh


[Post-Chorus]
Em          Bm
   I just wanna get her off, oh
Em Bm
    Oh
Em Bm      A
      Oh, oh
G F#m   Em
      Oh


[Verse 3]
                Bm
She's taking pictures in the mirror
         Em
Oh my God, her skin's so clear
           Bm
Tell her, "Bring that over here"
Em           Bm
   You need a seat? I'll volunteer
              A
Now she's smiling ear to ear
           G                 F#m
She's the headlights, I'm the deer


[Bridge]
Em                     Bm
  I've said it all before, but
I'll say it again
Em                    Bm
  I'm interested in more than
just being friends
Em               Bm
  I don't wanna break it, just
want it to bend
A                  G    F#m
 Do you know how to bend?


[Chorus]
Em          Bm
  I could eat that girl for lunch
Em      Bm
  She dances on my tongue
Em  Bm
  I know it's just a hunch
A                       G  F#m
 But she might be the one
```

```
[Outro]
Em       Bm Em
  I could
Bm
Eat that girl for lunch
Em          Bm A
   Yeah, she
               G                 F#m Em
Tastes like she might be the one
           Bm          Em
I could, I could
Bm                        Em
Eat that girl for lunch
           Bm          A
Yeah, she, yeah, she
               G                 F#m Bm
Tastes like she might be the one
```

When the Party's Over

Music by Billie Eilish

CHORDS

A   B   C#m   E   F#m   A#dim7

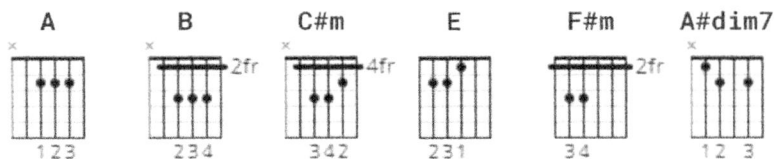

STRUMMING PATTERN

WHOLE SONG 62 bpm

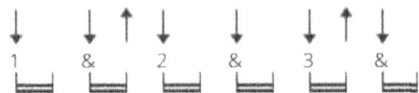

↓   ↓ ↑ ↓   ↓   ↓ ↑ ↓
1   &   2   &   3   &

[Intro]
A B C#m B E B A A B C#m B E B A

[Verse 1]
A   B   C#m B   E   B   A
Don't you know I'm no good for you?
         A   B C#m B   E
I've learned to lose you can't
B A
afford to
A   B   C#m   B E   B   A
Tore my shirt to stop you bleeding
      A B   C#m B E   B
But nothing e__ver stops you
A
leaving
                    A   B   C#m
Quiet when I'm coming home, I'm on
 B E
 my own

[Chorus]
F#m   C#m
I could lie and say I like it like
      E
 that, like it like that
F#m   C#m
I could lie and say I like it like
      E   A
 that, like it like that

[Verse 2]
A   B   C#m B   E   B A
Don't you know too much already?
       A B C#m B   E B   A
I'll only hurt you if you let me
A   B C#m   B   E   B   A
Call me friend, but keep me closer,
 call me back
            A   B   C#m B   E B
And I'll call you when the party's
A
over
                        A   B   C#m
Quiet when I'm coming home, I'm on
 B E
 my own

[Chorus]
     F#m   C#m
And I could lie and say I like it
          E
like that, like it like that
       F#m   C#m
Yeah, I could lie and say I like
              E   A
it like that, like it like that

[Bridge]

```
   E F#m          C#m           E      A
But   nothing is better, sometimes
E
F#m            C#m            E A
Once we both said our goodbyes
B                     A A#dim7
Let's just let it go
B               A
Let me let you go


[Outro]
                            C#m        E
Quiet when I'm coming home, I'm on
   A
my own
E  F#m                     C#m
   I  could lie and say I like it
          E              A
like that, like it like that
E  F#m                     C#m
   I  could lie and say I like it
          E              A
like that, like it like that
```

Everything I Wanted

Music by Billie Eilish

CHORDS

Dmaj7
5fr
3 2 4

E
7fr
2 3 4

C#m7
4fr
3 2

C#7
4fr
3 4

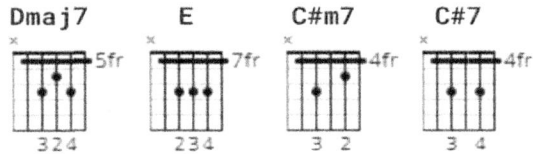

STRUMMING PATTERN

WHOLE SONG 120 bpm

↓   ↓ ↑   ↑ ↓   ↑ ↓   ↑ ↓   ↓ ↑   ↓   ↓   ↓ ↑
1 & 2 & 3 & 4 & 5 & 6 & 7 & 8 &

[Intro]
Dmaj7 E C#m7 Dmaj7 Dmaj7 E C#m7
Dmaj7

[Verse 1]
Dmaj7   E
   I had a dream
C#m7   Dmaj7
   I got everything I wanted
Dmaj7   E
   Not what you'd think
C#m7   Dmaj7
   And if I'm bein' honest
         Dmaj7   E
It might've been a nightmare
        C#m7   Dmaj7
To anyone who might care

[Verse 2]
Dmaj7   E
   Thought I could fly
C#m7   Dmaj7
   So I stepped off the Golden,
Dmaj7 E
   Nobody cried
C#m7   Dmaj7
   Nobody even noticed
        Dmaj7   E
I saw them standing right there
       C#m7   Dmaj7
Kinda thought they might care

[Pre-Chorus]
Dmaj7   E
   I had a dream
C#m7   Dmaj7
   I got everything I wanted
   Dmaj7   E
But when I wake up, I see
C#m7   Dmaj7
You with me

[Chorus]
        Dmaj7   E
And you say,   "As long as I'm
   C#m7   Dmaj7
here,   no one can hurt you
Dmaj7   E   C#m7
   Don't wanna lie here,   but
   Dmaj7
you can learn to
Dmaj7   E   C#7
   If I could change the way
   Dmaj7
that you   see yourself
Dmaj7   E
   You wouldn't wonder why you
  C#m7   Dmaj7
hear   they don't deserve you"

[Verse 3]

13

```
Dmaj7  E
     I tried to scream
C#m7                Dmaj7
     But my head was underwater
Dmaj7       E
     They called me weak
C#m7
     Like I'm not just
Dmaj7
somebody's daughter
              Dmaj7      E
Coulda been a nightmare
                         C#m7
But it felt like they were right
      Dmaj7
there


[Verse 4]
          Dmaj7                    E
And it feels like yesterday was a
year ago
      C#m7              Dmaj7
But I   don't wanna let anybody
know
          Dmaj7              E
'Cause everybody wants something
from me now
      C#m7                  Dmaj7
And I   don't wanna let 'em down


[Pre-Chorus]
Dmaj7  E
     I had a dream
C#m7            Dmaj7
     I got everything I wanted
     Dmaj7          E
But when I wake up, I see
C#m7        Dmaj7
You with me


[Chorus]
           Dmaj7            E
And you say,     "As long as I'm
     C#m7          Dmaj7
here,    no one can  hurt you
Dmaj7        E            C#m7
     Don't wanna lie here,    but
     Dmaj7
 you can  learn to
Dmaj7      E                  C#7
     If I could change the way
       Dmaj7
that you     see yourself
```

```
Dmaj7                    E
     You wouldn't wonder why you
  C#m7         Dmaj7
hear    they don't deserve you"


[Bridge]
Dmaj7            E
If   I knew it all then, would I do
          C#m7
 it again?
              Dmaj7
Would I do it again?
Dmaj7              E
If   they knew what they said would
              C#m7
 go straight to my head
              Dmaj7
What would they say instead?
Dmaj7            E
If   I knew it all then, would I do
       C#7
 it again?
            Dmaj7
Would I do it again?
Dmaj7              E
If   they knew what they said would
                 C#m7
 go straight to my head
              Dmaj7
What would they say instead?


[Outro]
Dmaj7
```

14

Ocean Eyes

Music by Billie Eilish

CHORDS

Cmaj7   G/D   Em   G   C

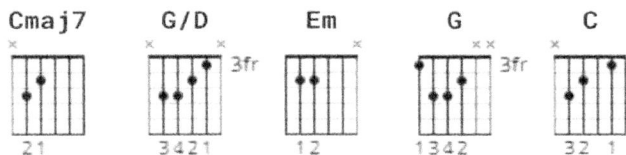

STRUMMING PATTERN

WHOLE SONG 145 bpm

1 & 2 & 3 & 4 & 5 & 6 & 7 & 8 &

[Intro]
Cmaj7 G/D Em Cmaj7 G/D Em Cmaj7 G/D
 Em G C

[Verse 1]
Cmaj7 G/D Em   Cmaj7 G/D
I've been watching you for   some
Em
time
Cmaj7 G/D Em   G
Can't stop staring at those ocean
C
eyes
Cmaj7 G/D Em   Cmaj7 G/D Em
Burn_ing cities and na___palm skies
Cmaj7 G/D Em   G
Fif__teen flares inside those ocean
 C
 eyes
      G   C
Your ocean eyes
No fair

[Chorus]
Cmaj7 G/D Em Cmaj7 G/D Em
          Cmaj7   G/D   Em
You really know how to make me cry
                    G   C
When you give me those ocean eyes
          Cmaj7 G/D Em Cmaj7 G/D Em
I'm scared

        Cmaj7   G/D
I've never fallen from quite this
Em
high
                    G   C
Falling into your ocean eyes
        G   C
Those ocean eyes

[Verse 2]
Cmaj7 G/D Em   Cmaj7
I've been walking through a world
G/D   Em
gone blind
Cmaj7 G/D Em   G
Can't stop thinking of your diamond
 C
 mind
Cmaj7 G/D Em   Cmaj7   G/D
Care_ful creature made friends with
 Em
 time
    Cmaj7 G/D Em   G
He left her lonely with a diamond
C
mind
            G   C
And those ocean eyes
No fair

[Chorus]

15

```
Cmaj7 G/D Em Cmaj7 G/D Em
           Cmaj7        G/D       Em
You really know how to make me cry
                         G       C
When you give me those ocean eyes
           Cmaj7 G/D Em Cmaj7 G/D Em
I'm scared
           Cmaj7        G/D
I've never fallen from quite this
Em
high
                    G      C
Falling into your ocean eyes
      G     C
Those ocean eyes


[Intrelude]
Cmaj7 G/D Em Cmaj7 G/D Em Cmaj7 G/D
 Em G C
Cmaj7 G/D Em Cmaj7 G/D Em Cmaj7 G/D
 Em G C
G C
No fair


[Outro]
Cmaj7 G/D Em Cmaj7 G/D Em
           Cmaj7        G/D       Em
You really know how to make me cry
                         G       C
When you give me those ocean eyes
           Cmaj7 G/D Em Cmaj7 G/D Em
I'm scared
           Cmaj7        G/D
I've never fallen from quite this
Em
high
                    G      C
Falling into your ocean eyes
      G     C
Those ocean eyes
```

Happier Than Ever

Music by Billie Eilish

CHORDS

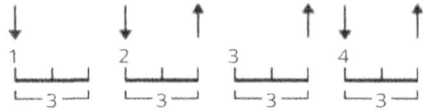

G	C	E7	Am	Dm7	G7	Fm	D	F

STRUMMING PATTERN

WHOLE SONG 91 bpm

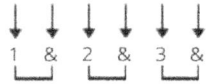

VERSE 2 80 bpm

[Intro]
```
G          C
 When I'm away from you
```

[Chorus]
```
                 E7
I'm happier than ever
                       Am
Wish I could explain it better
                 Dm7 G7
I wish it wasn't true
          C
Give me a day or two
```

[Verse 1]
```
                 E7
To think of something clever
                 Am
To write myself a letter
                 Dm7 G7 C
To tell me what to do
     C
Do you read my interviews?
     E7
Or do you skip my avenue?
```

```
         Am
When you said you were passin'
through
          Fm
Was I  even on your way?
       C
I knew when I asked you to
      E7
Be cool about what I was tellin'
you
            Am
You'd do the opposite of what you
said you'd do
            Fm
And I'd  end up more afraid
               E7
Don't say it isn't fair

You clearly weren't aware that you
Am          D
made me miserable, ooh
   Dm7                    G7
So if you really wanna know
             C
When I'm away from you
```

17

[Chorus]
```
              E7
I'm happier than ever
                          Am
Wish I could explain it better
               Dm7 G7 C
I wish it wasn't true
```

[Pre-Verse]
```
C E7 Am F Fm
```

[Verse 2]
```
C                    E7
 You call me again,  drunk in your
     Am
 Benz
              F           Fm      C
Drivin' home under the influence
                          E7
You scared me to death  but I'm
wastin' my breath
Am                    F
'Cause you only listen to your
     Fm
fuckin' friends
C                    E7
I don't relate to you
Am                   F
I don't relate to you, no
       Fm        C
'Cause I'd never treat me this
         E7
shitty
              Am              F
You made me hate this city
```

[Bridge]
```
                 C
And I don't talk shit about you on
    E7
the Internet
            Am              F
Never told anyone anything bad
                     C
'Cause that shit's embarrassing,
              E7
you were my everything
                  Am
And all that you did was make me
        F
fuckin' sad
```

```
       C
So don't waste the time I don't
E7
have
     Am                        F
And don't try to make me feel bad
                          C
I could talk about every time that
            E7
you showed up on time
                          Am
But I'd have an empty line 'cause
              F
you never did
                          C
Never paid any mind to my mother or
    E7
 friends, so I
                 Am
Shut 'em all out for you 'cause I
              F
was a kid
```

[Outro]
```
C                        E7
You ruined everything good
            Am                    F
Always said you were misunderstood
C                        E7
Made all my moments your own
Am                    F
Just fuckin' leave me alone
C E7 Am F
C E7 Am F
C E7 Am F
C E7 Am F
C
```

Bad Guy

Music by Billie Eilish

CHORDS

Gm   Cm   D

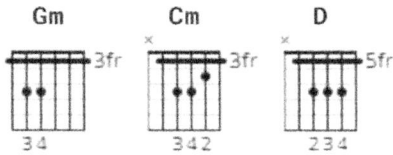

STRUMMING PATTERN

WHOLE SONG 136 bpm

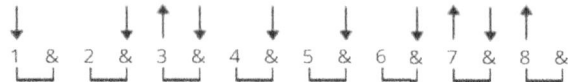

↓   ↓ ↑ ↓   ↓   ↓   ↓ ↑ ↓ ↑
1 & 2 & 3 & 4 & 5 & 6 & 7 & 8 &

[Intro]
Gm
Cm D

[Verse 1]
Gm
White shirt now red, my bloody nose
Sleepin', you're on your tippy toes
Cm
Creepin' around like no one knows
D
Think you're so criminal
Gm
Bruises on both my knees for you
Don't say thank you or please
       Cm
I do what I want when I'm wanting
to
D
My soul? So cynical
          Gm
So you're a tough guy

[Chorus]
Like it really rough guy
Just can't get enough guy
Chest always so puffed guy
         Cm
I'm that bad type
Make your mama sad type

                      D
Make your girlfriend mad tight
Might seduce your dad type
I'm the bad guy
Duh

[Bridge]
Gm   Cm   D
  I'm the bad guy

[Verse 2]
Gm
I like it when you take control
Even if you know that you don't
Cm
Own me, I'll let you play the role
D
I'll be your animal
Gm
My mommy likes to sing along with
me
But she won't sing this song
Cm
If she reads all the lyrics
        D
She'll pity the men I know
          Gm
So you're a tough guy

[Chorus]

Like it really rough guy
Just can't get enough guy
Chest always so puffed guy
        Cm
I'm that bad type
Make your mama sad type
                     D
Make your girlfriend mad tight
Might seduce your dad type
I'm the bad guy
Duh

[Bridge]
Gm   Cm   D   Gm
   I'm the bad guy, duh
                  Cm   D
I'm only good at bein' bad, bad

[Interlude]
Gm
   I like when you get mad
I guess I'm pretty glad that you're
 alone
You said she's scared of me?
I mean, I don't see what she sees
But maybe it's 'cause I'm wearing
your cologne

[Outro]
Gm
   I'm a bad guy
I'm a bad guy

20

My Future

Music by Billie Eilish

CHORDS

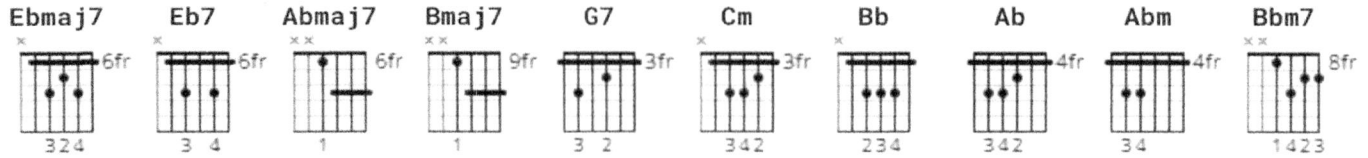

STRUMMING PATTERN

WHOLE SONG 105 bpm

[Verse 1]
```
   Ebmaj7
I can't seem to focus
        Eb7
And you don't seem to notice I'm
     Abmaj7
not here
          Bmaj7
I'm just a mirror
     Ebmaj7
You check your complexion
     Eb7
To find your reflection's all
      Abmaj7
alone
        Bmaj7
I had to   go
```

[Pre-Chorus]
```
G7
Can't you hear me?
Cm      Bb      Ab
I'm not coming home
Do you understand?
          Abm
I've changed   my plans
```

[Chorus]
```
        Ebmaj7       Eb7
'Cause I,    I'm in love
        Abmaj7
With my future
                     Bmaj7
Can't wait to meet      her
     Ebmaj7       Eb7
And I,    I'm in love
                    Abmaj7
But not with anybody else
                    Bmaj7       Ebmaj7
Just wanna get to know myself
```

[Verse 2]
```
Ebmaj7
      I know supposedly I'm lonely
now
Eb7
   Know I'm supposed to be unhappy
        Abmaj7
Without someone
          Bmaj7
But aren't I someone?
```

21

```
Bbm7 Ebmaj7 Eb7
      I'd    like to be your
Abmaj7
answer
                        Bmaj7 Dbm7
'Cause you're so handsome


[Pre-Chorus]
     G7
But I know better
Cm        Bb          Ab
Than to drive you  home
F                  Ab
 'Cause you'd invite me in
           Abm
And I'd be yours again


[Chorus]
       Ebmaj7        Eb7
'Cause I,    I'm in love
        Abmaj7
With my future
                   Bmaj7    Bbm7
And you don't know      her
    Ebmaj7        Eb7
And I,    I'm in love
                 Abmaj7
But not with anybody here
                 Bmaj7
I'll see you in a couple years
Ebmaj7
```

Ilomilo

Music by Billie Eilish

CHORDS

Fm **Cm** **Gm**

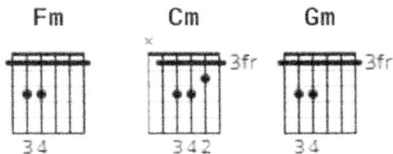

STRUMMING PATTERN

WHOLE SONG 120 bpm

↓   ↓ ↑   ↑ ↓ ↑
1 & 2 & 3 & 4 &

[Intro]
             Fm
Told you not to worry

[Verse 1]
             Cm
But maybe that's a lie
             Cm
Honey, what's your hurry?
          Gm
Won't you stay inside?
          Fm
Remember not to get too close to
stars

[Pre-Chorus]
             Cm
They're never gonna give you love
like ours

[Chorus]
Cm
Where did you go?
I should know, but it's cold
          Gm
And I don't wanna be lonely
So show me the way home
Fm   **Cm**
   I can't lose another life

[Bridge]
Cm   **Gm**
Hurry, I'm worried
                  Fm
The world's a little blurry

[Verse 2]
             Cm
Or maybe it's my eyes
                Cm
The friends I've had to bury
             Gm
They keep me up at night
                 Fm
Said I couldn't love someone

[Pre-Chorus]
'Cause I might break
             Cm
If you're gonna die, not by mistake

[Chorus]
    Cm
So, where did you go?
I should know, but it's cold
          Gm
And I don't wanna be lonely
So tell me you'll come home

23

```
Fm                          Cm
   Even if it's just a lie
                      Cm
I tried not to upset you


[Interlude]
                              Gm
Let you rescue me the day I met you
                      Fm
I just wanted to protect you
                      Cm
But now I'll never get to


[Bridge]
Cm          Gm      Fm Cm
Hurry, I'm worried


[Outro]
Cm
Where did you go?
I should know, but it's cold
              Gm
And I don't wanna be lonely
Was hoping you'd come home
Fm                        Cm Cm Gm
   I don't care if it's a lie
```

24

Your Power

Music by Billie Eilish

CHORDS

Fmaj7   Am   Em

STRUMMING PATTERN

WHOLE SONG 130 bpm

1 & 2 & 3 & 4 &

[Intro]
Fmaj7 Am Em Fmaj7 Am Em
Fmaj7 Am Em Fmaj7 Am Em

[Chorus]
Fmaj7   Am   Em
    Try not to abuse your power
Fmaj7   Am   Em
    I know we didn't choose to
change
Fmaj7   Am
    You might not wanna lose
    Em
your power
Fmaj7   Am
    But havin' it's so strange
Em

[Verse 1]
Fmaj7
She said you were a hero
Am   Em
You played the part
    Fmaj7
But you ruined her in a year
Am   Em
Don't act like it was hard
    Fmaj7
And you swear you didn't know
    Am   Em
No wonder why you didn't ask

    Fmaj7
She was sleepin' in your clothes
    Am   Em
But now she's got to get to class
    Fmaj7
How dare you?

[Pre-Chorus]
    Am Em
And how could you?
    Fmaj7
Will you only feel bad when they
find out?
    Am   Em
If you could take it all back
Would you?

[Chorus]
Fmaj7   Am   Em
    Try not to abuse your power
Fmaj7   Am   Em
    I know we didn't choose to
change
Fmaj7   Am
    You might not wanna lose
    Em
your power
Fmaj7   Am
    But havin' it's so strange
Em

[Verse 2]
Fmaj7
I   thought that I was special
Am   **Em**
You made me feel
               Fmaj7
Like it was my   fault, you were
the devil
Am   **Em**
Lost your appeal
        Fmaj7
Does it keep you in control?
              Am   **Em**
For you to keep her in a cage?
        Fmaj7
And you swear you didn't know
                   Am
You said you thought she was your
    Em
age
               Fmaj7
How dare you?

[Pre-Chorus]
                        Am Em
And how could you?
                       Fmaj7
Will you only feel bad if it turns
 out
                             Am   **Em**
That they kill your contract?
          Fmaj7
Would you?

[Chorus]
                      Am   **Em**
Try not to abuse your power
Fmaj7   **Am**   **Em**
    I know we didn't choose   to
    Fmaj7
change
                             Am
You might not wanna lose your
Em   **Fmaj7**
power
                        Am Em
But power isn't pain

[Outro]
Fmaj7 Am Em Fmaj7 Am Em
Fmaj7 Am Em Fmaj7 Am Em

Xanny

Music by Billie Eilish

CHORDS

A   E   Bm   Dm   F#m   Faug   A(b5)/Eb   E7

A — 1 2 3
E — 2 3 1
Bm — 2fr — 3 4 2
Dm — 2 3 1
F#m — 2fr — 3 4
Faug — 4 2 3 1
A(b5)/Eb — 4fr — 2 4 3 1
E7 — 2 1 3

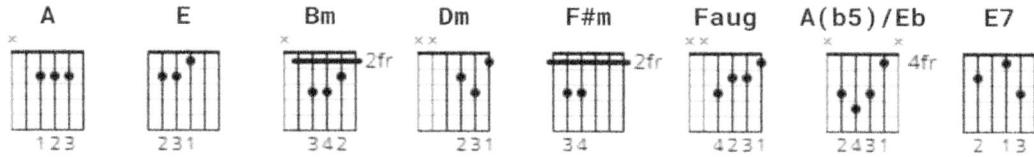

STRUMMING PATTERN

WHOLE SONG 55 bpm

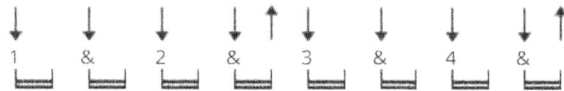

↓ ↓ ↓ ↓↑ ↓ ↓ ↓ ↓↑
1 & 2 & 3 & 4 &

[Verse 1]
       A
What is it about them?
       E
I must be missing something
         Bm
They just keep doing nothing
      Dm
Too intoxicated to be scared
       A
Better off without them
        E
They're nothing but unstable
        Bm
Bring ashtrays to the table
        Dm
And that's about the only thing
they share

[Chorus]
   F#m   Faug
I'm in their second hand smoke
A   A(b5)/Eb
Still just drinking canned Coke
Bm
I don't need a Xanny to feel better
   F#m   Faug
On designated drives home
A   A(b5)/Eb
Only one who's not   stoned
Bm
Don't give me a Xanny, now or ever

          A
Wakin' up at sundown

[Verse 2]
           E
They're late to every party
       Bm
Nobody's ever sorry
         Dm
Too inebriated now to dance
        A
Morning as they come down
          E
Their pretty heads are hurting
        Bm
They're awfully bad at learning
        Dm
Make the same mistakes, blame
circumstance

[Chorus]
   F#m   Faug
I'm in their second hand smoke
A   A(b5)/Eb
Still just drinking canned Coke
Bm
I don't need a Xanny to feel better
   F#m   Faug
On designated drives home
A   A(b5)/Eb
Only one who's not   stoned

```
Bm                              E
Don't give me a Xanny, now or ever
E7


[Interlude]
Bm
Please don't try to kiss me on the
E         E7
sidewalk
         F#m           Faug A
On your cigarette break
A(b5)/Eb
  Bm                            E
I can't afford to love someone
    E7          F#m       Faug
Who isn't dying by mistake    in
A             A(b5)/Eb
Silver Lake
Bm              A
  What is it about them?


[Outro]
                    E
I must be missing something
                        Bm
They just keep doin'  nothing
          Dm
Too intoxicated to be scared
A E Bm Dm A
            Come down
E
 Hurting
Bm          Dm
  Learning
```

28

Billie Bossa Nova

Music by Billie Eilish

CHORDS

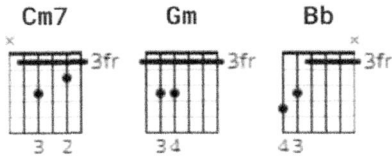

STRUMMING PATTERN

WHOLE SONG 110 bpm

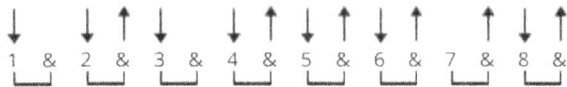

[Intro]
Cm7
Gm   **Cm7**
  Mmmmmm, mmmm
       Gm Bb
Nanana

Love when it comes without a
Cm7
warning

[Verse 1]

'Cause waiting for it gets so
Gm
boring
                Cm7
A lot can change in twenty seconds
           Gm Bb
A lot can happen in the dark

Love when it makes you lose your
Cm7
bearings
             Gm
Some information's not for sharing

Use different names at hotel
Cm7
checkins

                   Gm
It's hard to stop it once it starts
    Bb
 It starts

[Pre-Chorus]
Cm7
I'm not sentimental

But there's somethin' 'bout the way
             Gm
 you look tonight, mmm
            Cm7
Makes me wanna take a picture

Make a movie with you that we'd
        Gm   **Bb**
have to hide
                 Cm7
You better lock your phone

[Chorus]
                     Gm
And look at me when you're alone
                 Cm7
Won't take a lot to get you goin'
                Gm
I'm sorry if it's torture though I
      Bb
know, I know

29

```
                              Cm7
It might be more of an obsession


[Verse 2]
                                 Cm
You really make a strong impression
                        Cm7
Nobody saw me in the lobby
                              Gm          Bb
Nobody saw me in your arms, mmm


[Pre-Chorus]
Cm7
I'm not sentimental

But there's somethin' 'bout the way
            Gm
 you look tonight mmm
            Cm7
Makes me wanna make 'em jealous

I'm the only one who does it how
Gm          Bb
you like
                          Cm7
You better lock your phone


[Chorus]
                                    Gm
And look at me when you're alone
                               Cm7
Won't take a lot to get you goin'
                               Gm
I'm sorry if it's torture though  I
            Bb
 know, I know
                      Cm7
You better lock your door
                           Gm
And look at me a little more

We both know I'm worth waitin' for
Cm7
                               Gm
That heavy breathin' on the floor
                 Bb              Cm7
I'm yours, I'm yours I'm yours


[Solo Piano]
Gm Cm7 Gm Bb
```

```
[Fade Out]
Cm7
I'm not sentimental
Gm
I'm not sentimental
Cm7                         Gm Bb
I'm not sentimental
```

NDA

Music by Billie Eilish

CHORDS

Gm	Cm	Bb	Eb	D7	Gmmaj7	Csus2
3fr	3fr		6fr	5fr	3fr	3fr
3 4	3 4 2	2 3 4	2 3 4	3 4	3 2	3 4

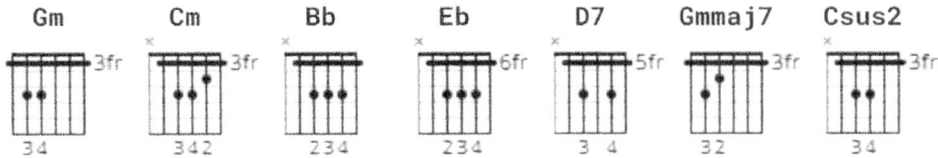

STRUMMING PATTERN

WHOLE SONG 85 bpm

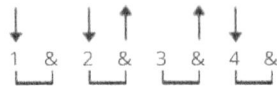

↓   ↓ ↑   ↑ ↓
1 & 2 & 3 & 4 &

[Verse 1]
      Gm
Did you think I'd show up in a
limousine? No
Had to save my money for security
Got a stalker walkin' up and down
the street
Says he's Satan and he'd like to
meet
       Cm
I bought a secret house when I was
seventeen
Haven't had a party since I got the
 keys
     Gm
Had a pretty boy over, but he
couldn't stay
On his way out I made him sign an
NDA, mm

[Pre-Chorus]
Gm
  Yeah, I made him sign an NDA
Cm
Once was good enough

'Cause I don't want him having shit
         Gm
 to sayay, ayy, ayy, ayyayy

Gm   Bb
  You couldn't save me, but you
       Eb Cm   Gm
can't let me go,   oh, no
                Bb
I can crave you, but you don't need
      Eb D7
 to know, ohoh

[Interlude]
Gm
Gmmaj7 Gm   Gmmaj7
     Mmmm, mmmm

[Verse 2]
Gm
Thirty under thirty for another
year
     Gmmaj7
I can barely go outside, I think I
hate it here
Gm
Maybe I should think about a new
career
Gmmaj7
Somewhere in Kaua'i where I can
disappear
        Cm
I've been havin' fun gettin' older
now

```
Csus2
Didn't change my number, made him
shut his mouth
    Gm
At least T gave him something he
can cry about
   Gmmaj7
I thought about my future, but I
                   Gm
want it now, ohoh


[Pre-Chorus]
           Gmmaj7 Gm      Gmmaj7
Want it now,            mmmmmm
Cm
You can't give me up
Csus2 Gm Gmmaj7


[Chorus]
Gm                               Bb
   You couldn't save me, but you
                Eb   Cm  Gm
can't let me go,  oh,  no
                             Bb
I can crave you, but you don't need
          Eb      D7
 to know,  ohoh
                        Gm
Did I take it too far?


[Bridge]
                      Bb
Now I know what you are
                Eb
You hit me so hard
        Cm
I saw stars
                       Gm
Think I took it too far
                     Bb
When I sold you my heart
                Eb
How'd it get so dark?
        D7
I saw stars


[Outro]
Gm
Stars
```

Blue

Music by Billie Eilish

CHORDS

C   Em   D   Am   Cm   G

32 1   12   1 32   2 31   342   3fr   21   34

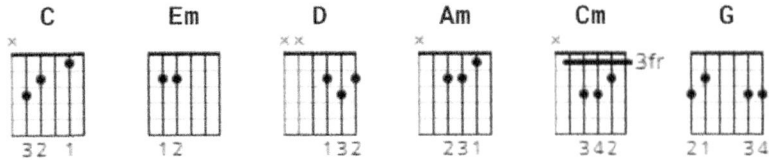

STRUMMING PATTERN

WHOLE SONG 105 bpm

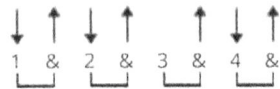

↓ ↑ ↓ ↑   ↑ ↓ ↑
1 & 2 & 3 & 4 &

[Intro]
C Em
 Mmm,
  D
Mmm
  Am
Mmm

[Chorus]
C Em   D
I try to live in black and white,
           Am
but I'm so blue
C Em   D
I'd like to mean it when I say I'm
     Am
over you
                    C   Em
But that's still not true, ooh
              D   Am
And I'm still so blue, oh

[Verse 1]
C   Em
I thought we were the same
            D   Am
Birds of a feather, now I'm ashamed
             C   Em
I told you a lie, desole, mon amour

                    D
I'm tryin' my best, don't know
                 Am
what's in store
                      C
Open up the door
                         Em
In the back of my mind, I'm still
          D
overseas
                      Am
A bird in a cage, thought you were
made for me

[Chorus]
C Em   D
I try to live in black and white,
           Am
but I'm so blue
But I'm not what you need
C Em   D
I'd like to mean it when I say I'm
     Am
over you
                         C   Em
But that's still not true, true
                 D
And I'm still so blue
          Am

33

[Interlude]
```
        C              Em
I'm true blue, true blue
            D   Am
I'm true blue
C    Em
  Mmm,
    D
Mmm
   Am
Mmm
    Cm        G
Aah, aah, aah
Aah
```

[Verse 2]
```
                Cm
You were born bluer than a
butterfly
                              G
Beautiful and so deprived of oxygen
Cm
Colder than your father's eyes

He never learned to sympathize with
  G
  anyone
          Cm
I don't blame you
```

[Chorus]
```
              G
But I can't change you
        Cm
Don't hate you
                G
But we can't save you
```

[Verse 3]
```
                  Cm
You were born reachin' for your
mother's hands

Victim of your father's plans to
G
rule the world
Cm
Too afraid to step outside
                          G
Paranoid and petrified of what
you've heard
```

```
                      Cm
But they could say the same 'bout
me
```

[Bridge]
```
I sleep 'bout three hours each
night
                                G
Means only twenty-one a week now,
now
                          Cm
And I could say the same 'bout you
Born blameless, grew up famous too
                          G
Just a baby born blue now, now
              Cm
I don't blame you
```

[Chorus]
```
              G
But I can't change you
        Cm
Don't hate you
                G
But we can't save you
```

[Post-Chorus]
```
Cm
   Aa-aa-aa, aa-aa-aa,
G
 Aaa, aaa
Cm                     G
   Aa-aa-aa, aa-aa-aa
```

[Outro]
```
 Cm    G
Aaa, aaa,
 Cm    G
Aaa, aaa,
Cm          G
  Aaa, aa, aa
```

The Diner

Music by Billie Eilish

CHORDS

```
   Bm          Em        F#sus4        F#
```

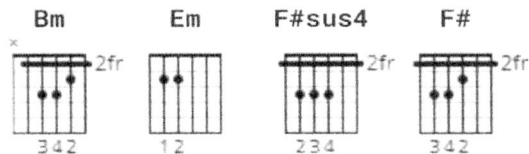

STRUMMING PATTERN

WHOLE SONG 125 bpm

```
↓    ↓ ↑    ↑ ↓ ↑
1 &  2 & 3 & 4 &
```

[Intro]
Bm

           Em
Don't be afraid of me
     F#sus4
I'm what you need
F#   Bm
  I saw you on the screens

[Verse 1]
I know we're meant to be
          Em
You're starring in my dreams

In magazines, you're looking right
  F#sus4
at me
F#   Bm
  I'm here around the clock
I'm waiting on your block
          Em
But please don't call the cops

They'll make me stop and I just
   F#sus4
wanna talk
F#   Bm
  Bet I could change your life

[Pre-Chorus]
You could be my wife

         Em
Could get into a fight
I'll say you're right
         F#
And you'll kiss me goodnight

[Chorus]
        Bm
I waited on the corner 'til I saw
the city leave
Was easy getting over and I landed
on my feet
         Em
I came in through the kitchen,
looking for something to eat
        F#
I left a calling card so they would
 know that it was me
Bm Em F#sus4 F#
      I tried to save you,
   Bm
 but I failed

[Verse 2]
Two fifty thousand dollar bail
         Em
While I'm away, don't read my mail
Just bring a veil
       F#sus4
And come visit me in jail

```
F#                          Bm
   I'll go back to the diner


[Pre-Chorus]
I'll write another letter
                          Em
I hope you'll read it this time
     F#
You better


[Chorus]
                     Bm
The cops around the corner, stopped
 me when I tried to leave
They told me I was crazy and they
knocked me off my feet
                          Em
They came in through the kitchen
looking for something discrete
                     F#
I left a calling card so they would
 know that it was me
Bm         Em
   It was me
    F#sus4
It was    me


[Outro]
F#                     Bm
   I memorized your number, now I
call you when I please
I tried to turn home, but now I'm
back up on my feet
                     Em
I saw you in the car with someone
else, they were asleep
                     F#
If something happens to me, can bet
 that you'll miss me
```

The 30th

Music by Billie Eilish

CHORDS

G   Gsus2/F#   Em   Am   D   C   Cmaj7   Em/B   Cm   Gaug

G6

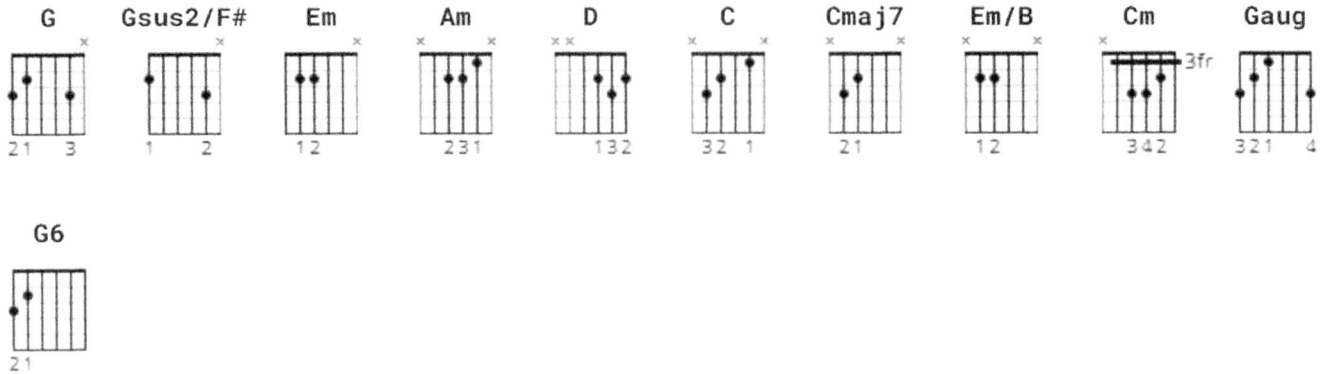

STRUMMING PATTERN

WHOLE SONG 72 bpm

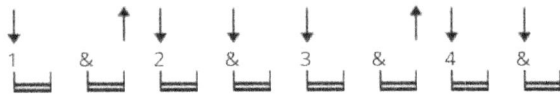

[Intro]
```
G Gsus2/F# Em Am G
D
```

[Verse 1]
```
G           Gsus2/F#
 Sometimes       you look the same
Em
                    Am
Just like you did  before the
  G
accident
D G         Gsus2/F#        Em
   When you're staring into space
                    Am
It's hard to believe  you don't
    G
remember it
    D
Woke up in the ambulance
```

[Pre-Chorus]

```
            Em              D
You pieced it all together on the
            C
drive
```

[Chorus]
```
   G              Em
I know you don't remember calling
   C
me
            G              Em
But I told you even then,  "You
            C
looked so pretty"
        Em       G       Cmaj7
In a hospital bed, I remember you
         Em/B
said
            Am              Cm
"You were scared, and so was I"
```

[Verse 2]
```
G         Gsus2/F#        Em
 In a standstill on the five
```

37

```
              Am           G
Thought it was unusual, the early
traffic
D                         G
Usually, I don't panic, I Just
       Gsus2/F#
wanted
          Em
to be on time
                    Am        G
When I saw the ambulances on the
shoulder
   D
I didn't even think of pulling over


[Pre-Chorus]
   Em                   D
I pieced it all together late that
      C
night


[Chorus]
          G                    Em
And I know you don't remember
          C
calling me
        G                    Em
But I told you even then,  "You
         C
looked so pretty"
        Em         G      Cmaj7
In a hospital bed, I remember you
    Em/B
said
              Am                Cm
"You were scared, and so was I"


[Bridge]
              G
What if it happened to you on a
   Gaug
different day?
            G6
On a bridge  where there wasn't a
   Gaug
rail    in the way?
          G
Or a neighborhood street where the
   Gaug
little kids play?
```

```
         G6
Or the Angeles Crest in the snow
Gaug
 or the rain?
                  G
What if you weren't alone? There
         Gaug
were kids    in the car
              G6
What if you  were remote? No one
      Gaug
knows    where you are
                      G
If you changed anything, would you
      Gaug
not    have survived?
              G6
You're alive,  you're alive, you're
        C
 alive


[Chorus]
        G                    Em
And I know you don't remember
          C
calling me
        G                    Em
But I told you even then,  "You
         C
looked so pretty"
                  Em        G
In your hospital bed, I remember
Cmaj7
you said
Em/B            Am
    "You were scared
Cm           G
  And so am I"
```

38

Oxytocin

Music by Billie Eilish

CHORDS

Em   C   B7

STRUMMING PATTERN

WHOLE SONG 125 bpm

```
[Intro]
Em


[Pre-Verse]
Em C B7 Em
C B7


[Verse 1]
Em
   Can't take it back once
            C        B7
It's been set in motion
Em C B7 Em
            You know I love
        C          B7
To rub it in like lotion
Em C B7          Em
      If you only


[Pre-Chorus]
            C  B7
Pray on Sunday
                Em
Could you come
            C  B7
My way on Monday?
                Em
'Cause I like  to
            C  B7
Do things God does
```

```
           Em
And improve  of
            C
If she saw us
      B7          Em
She couldn't look away,


[Chorus]
                  C
Look away, look away
      B7        Em
She'd wanna get involved,
                C
Involved, involved
      B7          Em
And what would people say,
                      C
People say, people say
        B7              Em
If they listen through the wall,
               C    B7
The wall, the wall?


[Verse 2]
Em                      C  B7
   I can see it clear as day
Em                       C  B7
   You don't really need to pray
Em                     C  B7
   Wanna see what you can take
```

39

```
Em                          C  B7
   You should really run away


[Bridge]
Em              C            B7
   I wanna do bad things to you
Em             C  B7
   I wanna make you yell
Em              C            B7
   I wanna do bad things to you
Em                  C  B7
   Don't wanna treat you well


[Verse 3]
Em
   Can't take it back once
          C     B7
It's been set in motion
Em C B7 Em
         You know I need
          C  B7
You for the Oxytocin


[Pre-Chorus]
Em C B7           Em
      If you find  it hard to
C  B7
swallow
          Em             C  B7
I can loosin' up your collar
              Em
'Cause as long  as
                C  B7
You're still breathin'
              Em
Don't you even
               C
Think of leavin'
        B7          Em
I kinda wanna look away,


[Chorus]
                   C
Look away, look away
     B7          Em
Kinda wanna get involved,
           C
Involved, involved
     B7             Em
And what would people say,
                   C
People say, people say
```

```
          B7
If they listen through
         Em                 C  B7
The wall, the wall, the wall?


[Verse 4]
Em                          C  B7
   I can see it clear as day
Em                           C  B7
   You don't really need to pray
Em                          C  B7
   Wanna see what you can take
Em                          C  B7
   You should really run away
Em                          C    B7
   Other people would have stayed
Em                      C  B7
   Other people don't obey
Em                            C  B7
   You and me are both the same
Em                          C  B7
   You should really run away
       Em
Bad things


[Outro]
C  B7 Em C  B7 Em
C  B7 Em C  B7
Em                 C            B7
   I wanna do bad things to you
Em              C  B7
   I wanna make you yell
Em               C            B7
   I wanna do bad things to you
Em                   C  B7
   Don't wanna treat you well
```

40

Male Fantasy

Music by Billie Eilish

CHORDS

Cadd9   G   D   Em7   Dsus4   Am7   G/B   Em   Dsus4/F#   C

D5

STRUMMING PATTERN

WHOLE SONG 111 bpm

↓ ↓ ↓ ↑ ↓ ↑
1 & 2 & 3 & 4 &

[Intro]
Cadd9
G D
Em7 Cadd9 G Dsus4
D

[Verse 1]
Cadd9   **G**
   Home alone, tryin' not to eat
D   **Em7**
 Distract myself   with pornography
Cadd9   **G**
   I hate the way she looks at me
D   **Cadd9**   **G**
 I can't stand the dialogue, she
                    D
would never be
                       Em7
That satisfied, it's a male fantasy
Cadd9   **G**
   I'm goin' back to therapy
D   **Am7**
 'Cause I loved you then

[Chorus]
              Em7
And I love   you now and I
 D   **Cadd9 G/B**
don't know how
                        Am7
Guess it's hard   to know
             Em7   **D**
When nobody else comes around
           Em Dsus4/F# G G/B C
If I'm getting   over you
       Em   **Dsus4/F# G G/B C**
Or just pre_____tending to
Em Dsus4/F# G   G/B C   G/B C
Be al_____right, convince my_self
D5 Em   **D**
I   hate you
Cadd9 G D Em7

[Verse 2]
Cadd9   **G**
   I got a call from a girl I
used to know

41

```
D            Em7
 We were inseparable   years ago
Cadd9
                        G
Thought we'd get along but it
        D
wasn't so
            Cadd9            G
And it's all    I think about
                        D
whÐµn I'm behind the wheel
              Em7
I worry this is how I'm always
D
gonna feel
Cadd9            G
   But nothing lasts, I know the
deal
D          Am7
 But I loved you then


[Chorus]
        Em7
And I love   you now and I
 D         Cadd9 G/B
don't know how
              Am7
Guess it's hard   to know
        Em7            D
When nobody else comes around
     Em Dsus4/F# G G/B C
If I'm getting    over  you
   Em   Dsus4/F# G G/B C
Or just pre_____tending to
Em Dsus4/F# G    G/B C    G/B C
Be al_____right, convince my_self
D5 Em   D
I  hate you
Em    Dsus4/F# G G/B C
Can't get     over  you
   Em Dsus4/F# G    G/B C
No matter     what I   do
  Em   Dsus4/F# G       G/B C G/B
I know I        should but I could
C D5 Em      D
never  hate you
```

42

Bittersuite

Music by Billie Eilish

CHORDS

F#m9 B/G# Amaj7 B C#m9 Bsus4 F#m C#m Dm9 E7

A7sus2 C Cmaj7 Em D Am

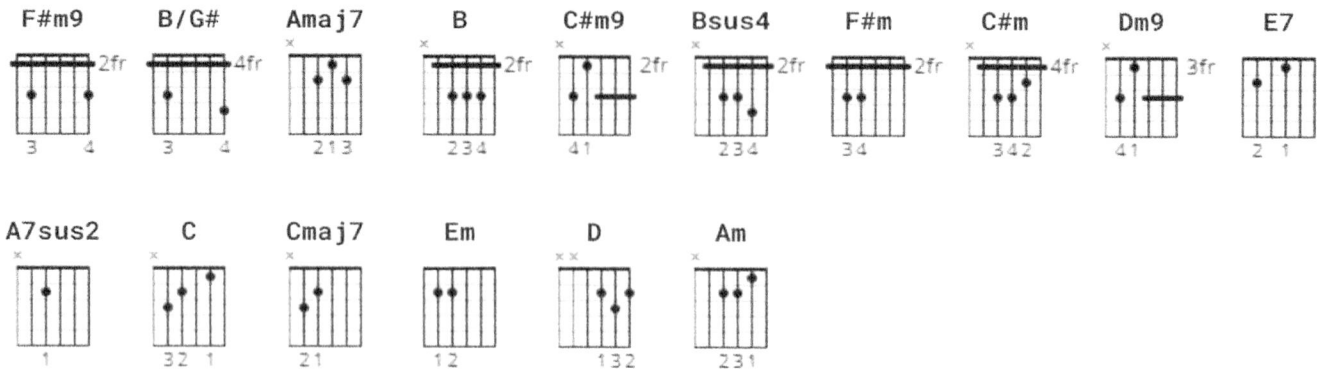

STRUMMING PATTERN

WHOLE SONG 75 bpm

[Part 1]
F#m9 B/G# Amaj7 B C#m9
B Bsus4
```
F#m9          B/G# Amaj7    B      C#m9
   I can't fall in    love with
     B
you
              F#m
I've been overseas
```

[Verse 1]
```
I've been havin' dreams
              C#m
You were in the foyer
I was on my knees
              F#m
Outside of my body
Watchin' from above
                  C#m
I see the way you want me
I wanna be the one
```

[Pre-Chorus]
```
F#m9                   B/G#
   But I gotta be careful
```

```
Amaj7                    B
   Gotta watch what I say
C#m9                          B
   God, I hope it all goes away
```

[Chorus]
```
        F#m9              B/G#  Amaj7
'Cause    I can't fall    in
         B    C#m9 B
love with you
   F#m9              B/G#   Amaj7 B
No    matter how    bad       I
want to
```

[Part 2]
Dm9 E7 A7sus2 C

[Chorus]
```
Dm9                 E7
   I don't need to breathe when
you look at me, all I see is
green
```

```
        A7sus2                                  C
And I think that we're in between    We can be discrete
everything I've seen                               Dm9
        C                            But I've been overseas
In my dream, have it once a week,
can't land on my feet
        Dm9                          [Verse 3]
Can't sleep, have you underneath                   E7
all of my beliefs                    And I've been havin' dreams
        E7                                   A7sus2
Keep it brief                        L'amour de ma        vie
                A7sus2                       C
I'll wait in the suite               Love so bittersweet, mm
        C                                    Dm9              E7
Keep me off my feet                  Open up the door for me, for  me
                                                     A7sus2
                                     'Cause I'm still on my       knees
[Verse 2]                                    C
Dm9                                  I'm stayin' off my feet
    You seem so paranoid
E7
    I'm looking at the  boys         [Bridge]
A7sus2                               Cmaj7 Em Cmaj7 Em
        I've never filled the void   D Am
C
 Out of spite
Dm9                                  [Outro]
    You seem so paralyzed            Cmaj7 Em D Am
E7                                   Cmaj7 Em D Am
    It's so romanticized             Cmaj7 Em D Am
A7sus2
        If this is how I die
C
 That's alright
                Dm9
I've been overseas


[Chorus]
                E7
I don't need to breathe when you
look at me, all I see is green
        A7sus2
And I think that we're in between
everything I've seen
        C
In my dream, have it once a week,
can't land on my feet
        Dm9
Can't sleep, have you underneath
all of my beliefs
        E7
Keep it brief
                A7sus2
I'll see you in the suite
```

When I Was Older

Music by Billie Eilish

CHORDS

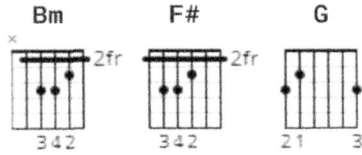

[Intro]
Bm F# G F#

[Chorus]
Bm

　　　　F#
When I was older

　　　G　　　　　　　　**F#**
I was a sailor on an open sea
Bm　　　　　　　　　**F#**
　But now I'm underwater

　　　　　　G
And my skin is paler than it should

　　　F#
　ever be

Hmm

[Interlude]
Bm

[Verse]
Bm
　I'm on my back again
F#
　Dreaming of a time and place

　　　　　　G
Where you and I remain the best of
friends
Even after all this ends
F#
　Can we pretend?
Bm
　I'm on my, I'm on my back again
F#
　It's seeming more and more

　　　　　　　G
Like all we ever do is see how far
it bends
Before it breaks in half and then

F#
　We bend it back again

[Pre Chorus]
Bm
Guess I got caught in the middle of
 it
Yes I've been taught, got a little
of it

　　　　　　　F#
In my blood,　in my blood
G
Memories burn like a forest fire
Heavy rain turns any funeral pyre
to mud
F#
　In the flood

[Chorus]
Bm　　　　　**F#**
　When I was older

　　　　　　G　　　　　　　**F#**
I was a sailor on an open sea
Bm　　　　　　　　　**F#**
　But now I'm underwater

　　　　　　G
And my skin is paler than it should

　　　F#
　ever be

[Bridge]
Bm
　I'm watching movies back to back
in black and white, I never
Seen anybody do it like I do it any
 better
F#
　Been goin' over you, I'm
overdue for new endeavors

45

Nobody lonely like I'm lonely and I
 don't know whether
G
 You'd really like it in the
 limelight
You'd sympathize with all the bad
guys
F#
  I'm still a victim in my own
right
But I'm the villain in my own eyes,
 yeah

[Outro]
Bm   F#
  When I was older
          G   F#
I was a sailor on an open sea

Lo Vas A Olvidar

Music by Billie Eilish

CHORDS

Em   G   C   D

STRUMMING PATTERN

WHOLE SONG 92 bpm

↓   ↓ ↑   ↓
1 & 2 & 3 & 4 &

[Verse 1]
```
Em                    G      C
Dime si me echas de menos aun
D Em              G      C
   Dime si no me perdonas aun
```

[Pre-Chorus]
```
D    Em                    G
  Que  haras con to' este veneno?
            C
Na' bueno
D Em                  G      C
   Dime si me echas de menos aun
```

[Chorus]
```
D    Em
  Lo vas a olvidar
                G
Can you let it go?
Can you let it go?
  C
Lo vas a olvidar
                D
Can you let it go?
Lo vas a olvidar
  Em
Lo vas a olvidar
                G
Can you let it go?
```

```
Can you let it go?
  C
Lo vas a olvidar
                        D
Can you let it go?
Lo vas a olvidar
```

[Bridge]
Em G C D

[Verse 2]
```
Em                    G      C D Em
Dime que no te arrepientes a_un
                      G        C D
Dime si aun queda algo en comun
```

[Pre-Chorus]
```
Em                G      C  D Em
El tiempo que se pierde no vuel_ve
                       G        C D
Dame un beso y bajame de la cruz
```

[Chorus]
```
Em
Lo vas a olvidar
                G
Can you let it go?
```

47

Can you let it go?
C
Lo vas a olvidar
              D
Can you let it go?
Lo vas a olvidar
Em
Lo vas a olvidar
              G
Can you let it go?
Can you let it go?
C
Lo vas a olvidar
              D
Can you let it go?
Lo vas a olvidar

[Outro]
Em G C D Em
                    G
El amor no puede medirse en paso
      C
firme
                          D
Un dia se hundio y al otro no puedo
        Em
 partirme
                  G
I needed to go cuz I needed to know
                      C
 you don't need me
                      D
You reap what you sow, but it seems
                        Em
 like you don't even see me
              G
El amor no puede medirse en paso
    C
firme
            D
Un dia se hundio y al otro no puedo
          Em
 partirme
                    G
You say it to me like it's

something I have any choice
    C
 in
                    D
If I wasn't important, then why
would you waste all your poi

Goldwing

Music by Billie Eilish

CHORDS

Amaj7	G#m7	F#m7	E	A6	C#m/A	A	C7	Bbmaj7	C7/Bb

Am7	C	Am	Dm	Gm7

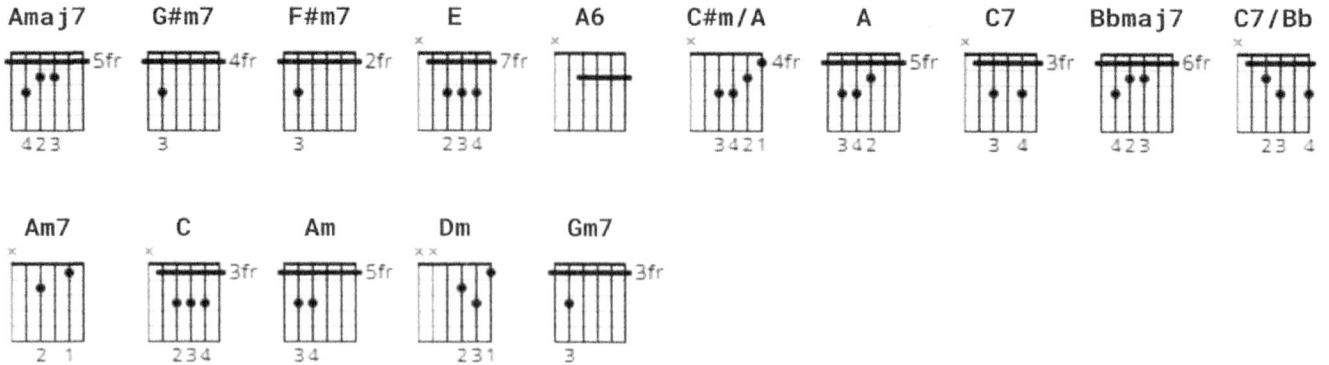

STRUMMING PATTERN

WHOLE SONG 160 bpm

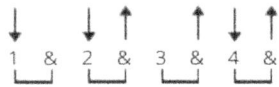

↓   ↓ ↑   ↑ ↓ ↑
1 & 2 & 3 & 4 &

```
[Intro]
Amaj7      G#m7        F#m7
"He   hath come to the bosom of his
   E
beloved
Amaj7      G#m7       F#m7      A6
Smiling on him, she beareth him to
C#m/A A  C7
high_est heav'n
Bbmaj7          C7/Bb
With   yearning heart"
Bbmaj7          C7/Bb
"On   thee we gaze, O' goldwing'd
Am7            C   Am E    Dm
messenger of mighty Gods"


[Verse 1]
Dm
  Goldwing angel
Go home, don't tell
Anyone what you are
You're sacred and they're starved
And their art is gettin' dark
And there you are to tear apart
Tear apart, tear apart, tear apart
```

```
                       Bbmaj7
You better keep your head downdown


[Chorus]
  Gm7            Dm
Dadadowndown, dadadowndown
                        Bbmaj7
Better keep your head downdown
  Gm7            Dm
Dadadowndown, dadadowndown


[Verse 2]
                Dm
They're gonna tell you what you
wanna hear
Then they're gonna disappear
Gonna claim you like a souvenir
Just to sell you in a year
                       Bbmaj7
You better keep your head downdown


[Chorus]
  Gm7            Dm
Dadadowndown, dadadowndown
```

49

                     Bbmaj7
Keep your head downdown
     Gm7   **Dm**
Dadadowndown, dadadowndown
                          Bbmaj7
Better keep your head downdown
     Gm7   **Dm**
Dadadowndown, dadadowndown
                     Bbmaj7
Keep your head downdown
     Gm7   **Dm**
Dadadowndown, dadadowndown
That's good!

Everybody Dies

Music by Billie Eilish

CHORDS

Eb	F	Bb	Gm	Cm	Dm
x 6fr	.....	x	..... 3fr	x 3fr	x x ....
2 3 4	3 4 2	2 3 4	3 4	3 4 2	2 3 1

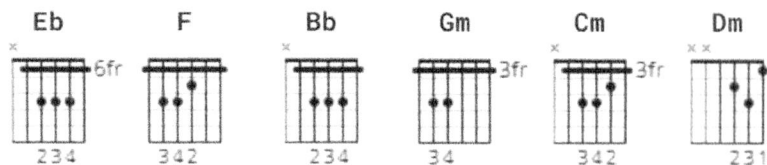

STRUMMING PATTERN

WHOLE SONG 65 bpm

↓   ↓   ↓   ↓ ↑
1 & 2 & 3 & 4 &

[Intro]
Eb F
Bb Gm   Eb   F
      Everybody dies, surprise,
surprise

[Verse 1]
                         Bb
We tell each other lies, sometimes,
Gm
   we try
                      Cm
To make it feel like we might be
       F
right
We might not be alone

[Chorus]
Gm F Eb
          Gm F
Be alone

[Verse 2]
Eb   Eb
   "Everybody dies," that's what
   F
they say

                              Bb
And maybe, in a couple hundred
                      Gm
years, they'll find another way
                      Cm   F
I just wonder why you'd wanna stay
If everybody goes

[Chorus]
Gm F Eb
                         Gm F
You'd still be alone
Eb   Gm
  I don't wanna cry, some days I
      F
do

[Bridge]
                    Eb
But not about you
                      Gm   F
It's just a lot to think about
                      Eb
The world I'm used to
            Cm   Gm
The one I can't get back, at
F   Eb
lĐμast not for a while

51

```
                    Gm
I sure have a knack  for seein'
     F                Eb
lifÐµ more like a child
                   Gm
It's not my fault,  it's not so
     F                Eb
wrong to wonder why
Dm              Cm
Everybody dies,  and when will I?


[Verse 3]
Eb                 F
   You oughta know
                        Bb
That even when it's  time, you
Gm
might not wanna go
                 Cm
But it's okay  to cry and it's
                     F
alright to fall
But you are not alone


[Outro]
Gm F Eb
                   Gm     F
You are not unknown
Eb Gm F Eb Gm F
Eb Eb F Bb
Gm
```

Not My Responsibility

Music by Billie Eilish

CHORDS

```
C#m7      G#7sus2
```

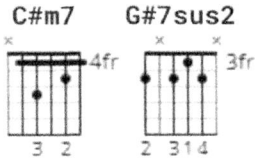

STRUMMING PATTERN

WHOLE SONG 58 bpm

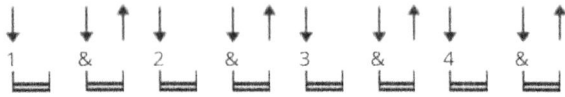

```
↓     ↓ ↑ ↓   ↓ ↑ ↓   ↓ ↑ ↓   ↓ ↑
1     &   2   &   3   &   4   &
```

[Intro]
C#m7 G#7sus2 C#m7 G#7sus2

[Verse 1]
C#m7
        G#7sus2
Do you know   me?
Really know me?
C#m7   G#7sus2
    You have opinions about my
opinions
C#m7
About my music
About my clothes
G#7sus2
        About   my   body
        C#m7
Some people   hate   what I wear
Some people praise it
            G#7sus2
Some   people use   it to shame
others
Some people use it to   shame   me
        C#m7
But   I feel you   watching
Always
    G#7sus2
And nothing I   do goes unseen

So while I feel your stares, your
            C#m7
disapproval or your sigh of
relief
If I lived by them, I'd never be
able to move
            G#7sus2
Would you like   me to be smaller,
weaker, softer, taller?
            C#m7
Would you like me to be quiet?
Do my shoulders provoke you? Does
my chest?
G#7sus2
        Am I my stomach? My hips?
The body I was born with
C#m7
    Is it not what you wanted?

If I wear what is comfortable,
G#7sus2
  I am not a woman
                    C#m7
If I shed the layers,   I'm a slut

Though you've never seen my body,
    G#7sus2
you still judge it
And judge me for it
Why?

53

C#m7
    We make assumptions about
people based on their size
            G#7sus2
We decide who   they are
We decide what they're worth
               C#m7
If I wear more,   if I wear less
Who decides what that makes me,
what that means?
     G#7sus2
Is my value based only on your
perception?
                         C#m7
Or is your opinion of me not my
responsibility?

OverHeated

Music by Billie Eilish

CHORDS

G#madd9   C#m7

STRUMMING PATTERN

WHOLE SONG 115 bpm

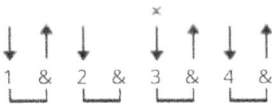

↓ ↑ ↓   ↓ ↑ ↑ ↓ ↑
1 & 2 & 3 & 4 &

[Intro]
G#madd9

I don't really even know how it
  C#m7
happened

[Verse 1]
I started talking, they started
laughing

I don't really even know how it
  G#madd9
happened
I started watching them
photographing
        C#m7
I don't really how it happened

[Pre-Chorus]
Instead of stopping, they still
were flashing
I started walking
    G#madd9
Gave no reaction, no reaction

[Chorus]
    C#m7
I'm overheated, can't be defeated

Can't be deleted, can't unrelievÐµ
It
    G#madd9
I'm overheated, can't be defeated
Can't be deleted, can't be repeated

[Interlude]
    C#m7   **G#madd9**
I'm overheated, I'm overheated

I don't really wanna know why you
    C#m7
went   there

[Verse 2]
I kinda don't care
You wanna kill me
You wanna hurt me
    G#madd9
Stop being flirty, hehehehehehehe
It's kinda working, hahaha

[Pre-Chorus]
    C#m7
Ha, did you really think this is
the right thing to do?
Is It news? News to who?
    G#madd9
That I really looked just like
the rest of you

[Chorus]
         C#m7
I'm overheated, can't be defeated
Can't be deleted, can't unrelievÐµ
It
         G#madd9
I'm overheated, can't be defeated
Can't be deleted, can't be repeated

[Post-Chorus]
    C#m7
And everybody said it was a let
down
I was only built like everybody
else now
But I didn't get a surgery to help
out
Because I'm not about to redesign
myself now
    G#madd9
Am I?   Am I? Am I?
            C#m7
All these other inanimate bitches

[Bridge]
It's none of my business
But don't you get sick of

Posing for pictures with that
G#madd9
 plastic body?
Man...

[Chorus]
         C#m7
I'm overheated, can't be defeated
Can't be deleted, can't unrelievÐµ
It
         G#madd9
I'm overheated, can't be defeated
Can't be deleted, can't be repeated
         C#m7
I'm overheated

[Outro]
G#madd9 C#m7 G#madd9

56

L'Amour de Ma Vie

Music by Billie Eilish

CHORDS

Bm   E   A   C#m   F#   F#m   E/G#   Bm7   E7   Amaj7

C#m7   F#m7   C   D   Em   G

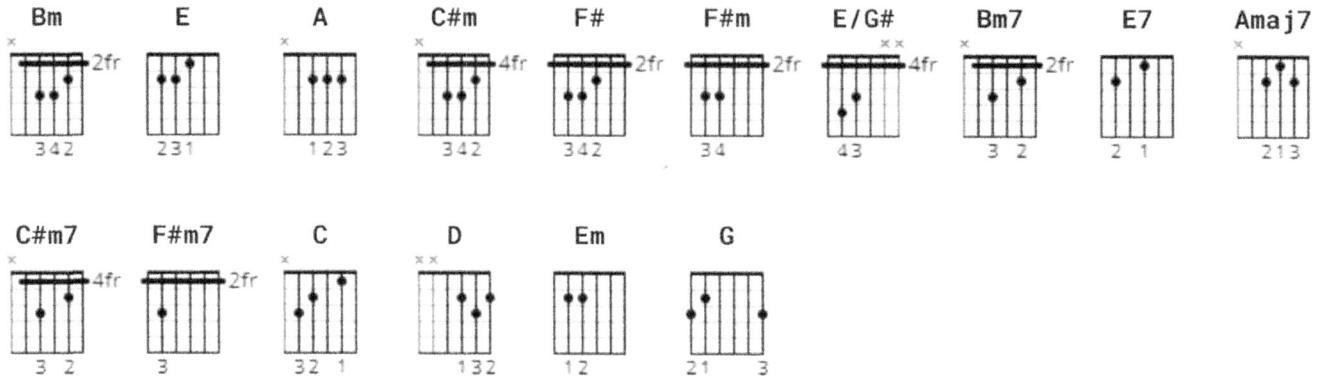

[Chorus]
```
Bm                          E
   I wish you the best for the rest
               A
of your life
      C#m            F#
Felt sorry for you  when I looked
              Bm
in your eyes
                          E
But I need to confess, I told you a
     A C#m F#m
 lie
          Bm E
I said you
A   C#m F#m
You       were the love of my life
Bm
E                         A E
  The love of my life
A                          F#m
 Did I break your heart?
```

[Verse 1]
```
Bm                          E
   Did I waste your time?
A  C#m               F#m
 I tried to be there   for you
Bm            E           A C#m
  Then you tried to break mine
```

[Bridge]

```
              F#m
It isn't asking for a lot for an
    Bm
apology
            E
For making me feel like it'd kill
         A          C#m
you if I tried to leave
                F#m
You said you'd never fall in love
            Bm
again because  of me
                 E    C#m
Then you moved on immediately (Bum,
        Bm
 bum, bum)
```

[Chorus]
```
                         E
But I wish you the best for the
                 A
rest of your life
      C#m          F#m
Felt sorry for you   when I looked
             Bm
in your eyes
                          E
But I need to confess, I told you a
    A C#m F#m
 lie
              Bm E
When I said you
```

57

```
      A C#m F#m                                    F#m
You        were the love of my           You said you'd never fall in love
   Bm                                               Bm
life                                     again because  of me
E                       A E                                        E
 The love of my life                     Then you moved on, then you moved
                                         on


[Verse 2]
A   E/G#          F#m                     [Bridge]
 So you found her,   now go fall in      Then you moved on, then you moved
      Bm                                 on
 love                                    Then you moved on, then you moved
                 E           A           on
Just like we were if I ever was          Bm C D E
      C#m          F#m                   Bm C D E
It's not my fault,   I did what I
      Bm
could                                    [Verse 3]
                E                        Em
You made it so hard like I knew you      Ooh
      C#m                                You wanted to keep it
 would                                                            G
                                         Like somethin' you found
                                         C
[Interlude]                               'Til you didn't need it
Bm7                         E7           Em
    Thought I was depressed  or             But you should've seen it
           Amaj7                                                G
losing my mind                           The way it went down
    C#m7          F#m7                    C
My stomach upset   almost all of          Wouldn't believe it
         Bm7                             Em
the time                                    Wanna know what I told her
                E7                                       G
But after I left,  it was obvious        With her hand on my shoulder?
 Amaj7 C#m7       F#m7                    C
 why       (Oh),  mm                      You were so mediocre
            Bm7     E7 Amaj7 C#m7         Em                        Bm C
Because for  you,   you                     And we're so glad it's over now
F#m7                                     D
                          Bm7            E           Bm C D
I was the love of your life,   mm         It's over now
E7                        A E            E           Bm C D
  But you were not mine                   It's over now
A        F#m                             E           Bm C D E
 It isn't asking for a lot for an         It's over now
    Bm
 apology
            E                            [Outro]
For making me feel like it'd kill        Em
        A           C#m                  Camera
you if I tried to leave                  Caught on camera
                                         The girls on camera
                                         Your girl's a fan of
                                         Miss me
```

Printed in Dunstable, United Kingdom

75462497R00040